Big Brutus

the Kansas Coal Shovel

Written by Brenda Eck   Illustrated by Jessie Pohl

To Jill
Brenda Eck

Rowe Publishing

To my cousin Marilyn.

Even when we were kids,

you had the best ideas.

This book was a great one.

~~~~~~~~~~

ISBN 13: 978-1-939054-33-3
ISBN 10: 1-939054-33-8

Illustrations by Jessie Pohl
Photos courtesy of Janet Britt, Mike Isakson, and Tom Ward

1 3 5 7 9 8 6 4 2

Printed in the United States of America
Published by

Rowe Publishing

www.rowepub.com
Stockton, Kansas

In a small field in Kansas
Flanked by trees and low hills,
See the mighty Big Brutus
Standing silent and still.

Long ago he worked hard
At this very site;
He dug in the coal mines
Both the day and the night.

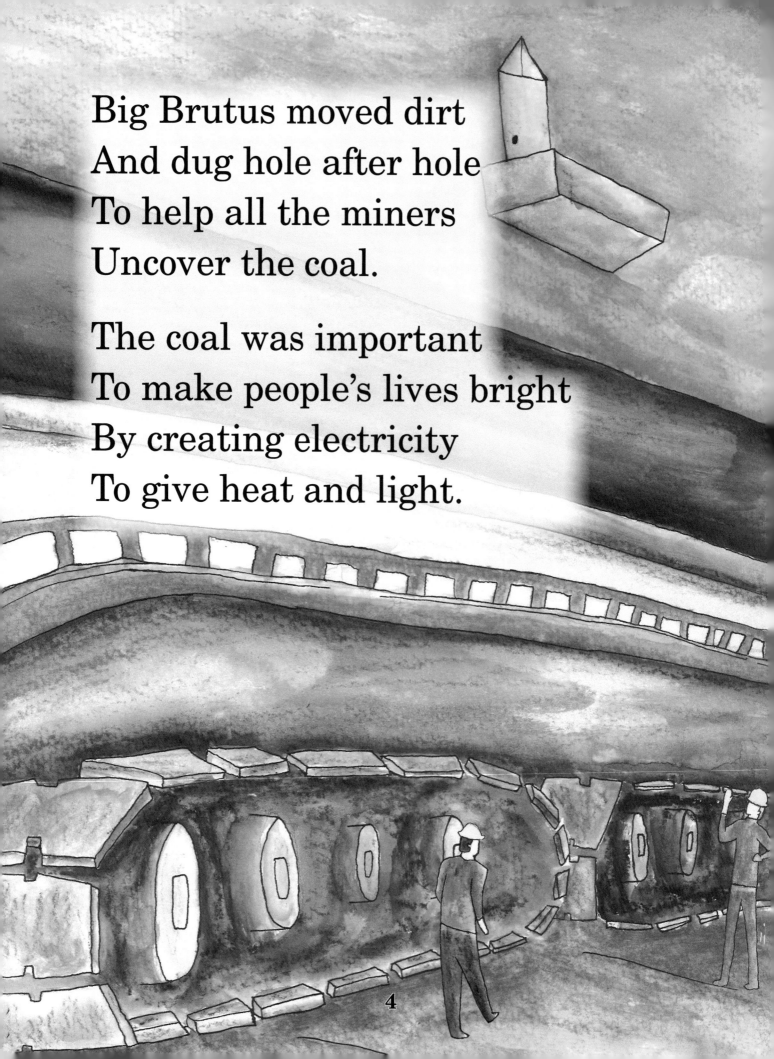

Big Brutus moved dirt
And dug hole after hole
To help all the miners
Uncover the coal.

The coal was important
To make people's lives bright
By creating electricity
To give heat and light.

4

But then it all changed;
The Kansas coal in the ground
Cost too much to mine;
Our coal shovel shut down.

Other jobs for Big Brutus
Were too far away;
He was too big to move,
So here he would stay.

What would happen to him?
Would he be covered with dust?
Would he sit here forever
Just to age and to rust?

Such a great, mighty machine
With so much power and pride—
What a shame if our shovel
Were shoved to the side.

For a while that's what happened.
He sat sad and alone
While the birds and the beasts
Used Big Brutus for homes.

Then the people who loved him
Came up with a plan;
We'd keep Brutus with us
Right where he began.

But we'd give him the honor
That we knew he deserved.
He'd be a museum,
His history preserved.

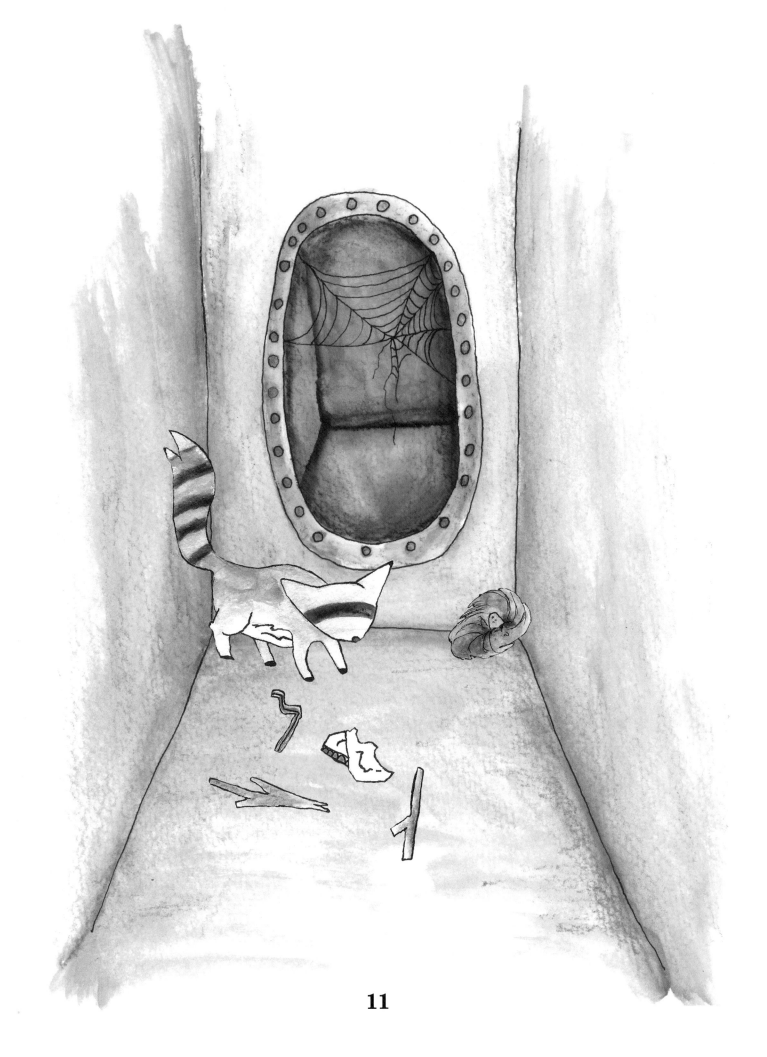

Kids would climb up his steps
And sit high in the air.

They could see half of Kansas
From his driver's chair.

They could crawl in his crawlers,
His insides, explore,
And in giant Big Brutus
Imaginations would soar.

His great gears would amaze them,
'Round his cables they'd run,
And instead of the silence
There'd be laughter and fun.

We would tell the great story
Here where Big Brutus stands
Of the men and machines
Who brought light to the land.

Now others would know him.
This would be a fit shrine
For Big Brutus, the coal shovel,
And the men in the mines.

So Brutus still stands here
That others might know
This tower of power
From long, long ago.

Big Brutus Facts:

- Designed and built by Bucyrus-Erie for the Pittsburg & Midway (P&M) Coal Mining Company

- 150 railroad cars were needed to bring all the parts

- Bucyrus Erie Model 1850B is the only one of its kind ever built

- Largest electric shovel in the world

- 16 stories tall (160 feet)

- Weighs 11 million pounds

- Boom is 150 feet long

- Dipper capacity 90 cu. yds (by heaping, 150 tons—enough to fill three railroad cars)

- Maximum speed .22 MPH

- Cost $6.5 million (in 1962)

On July 13, 1985, Big Brutus was dedicated as "a Museum and Memorial Dedicated to the Rich Coal Mining History in Southeast Kansas."

In September 1987, the American Society of Mechanical Engineers (ASME) designated Big Brutus a Regional Historic Mechanical Engineering Landmark, the 10th since 1971 to be so designated.

Big Brutus is a museum open year round. Hours vary with the season. Visit www.bigbrutus.org or call (620) 827-6177 for more information.

CPSIA information can be obtained
at www.ICGtesting.com
Printed in the USA
406657LV00001B/4

9 781939 054333